yes with variations

by

Ken McLaren

Edited with an
introduction by

William Packard

The Smith   New York

A New York Quarterly Book

Composed in Univers, with variant settings in Arthur Bold, Bookman Bold Italic, Chelsea, Fancy Pants, Helvetica, Imperial Roman, Lazybones, Libra, Olde English, Period, Pretorian and Stylized Gothic.

Copyright © 1983 by the estate of Ken McLaren

ISBN Number: 0-939196-00-X

Composition by Marjorie Finnell.
Lay-out and design by William Packard.
Cover photograph by Ken McLaren.
Printed by Capital City Press

CONTENTS

KEN McLAREN died in June, 1979, leaving behind innumerable poems in notebooks, journals, napkins, scraps of paper, and recorded on cassettes. These poems are a wild jumble of words on love, sex, kindness, friendship, minorities, asshole politicos, lots of "Betty poems," poems on poetry itself, and poems on the importance of having a happy attitude towards oneself and the rest of the world.

Ken's friends had been urging him for years to sort through his writings and get a collection together for publication. But Ken was always too busy speaking out against callous bureaucracies and the worst excesses of the established social, political, and sexual order. Ken saw himself as a voice for the voiceless, so the closest he ever got to sorting through his own poetry was when he had to do a poetry reading for some cause like the peace movement or civil rights or gay liberation or the Gray Panthers or CORE or the Living Theatre or for any one of a hundred other causes.

So this is the first real collection of Ken McLaren's poems to be published, and it's too bad that Ken won't be able to hold the book in his own hands and then go reading through it and then chuckle amiably about how some things do work out okay in this world after all.

* * *

* * *

*J*UNE 18, 1979. There is a memorial service for Ken McLaren at the United Methodist Church on West 4th Street in Greenwich Village in New York. At 3:00 P.M. it begins to thunder and lightning, and then it rains, and the rain cools everything off. The way Ken himself liked to cool everything off. Someone named Greg from the Gray Panthers is up at the lectern and is talking about how Ken McLaren lived his life:

> *He is a fallen comrade in the fight to humanize the*
> *world—to make human beings of blacks, of the poor,*
> *of the gays, of women, of people who live near*
> *nuclear power plants—*

AND THEN I get up and I try to tell how Ken McLaren was in the very first poetry writing class I taught at New York University, in the early 1960's. It was supposed to be Louise Bogan's class, but Miss Bogan was ill, so I had been hired to teach the writing class in her absence. Warren Bower explained the situation to the class, and then he introduced me to the class, and there were audible groans of disappointment because most of the students had signed up to work with Louise Bogan. But then a voice spoke up from the rear of the class: "Stop your groaning and let's give this young man a chance!"

THAT WAS Ken McLaren—his vivid sense of fair play and his instinct for social justice and his openness to whatever might happen to come along. And Ken kept coming back to register for my writing class at NYU, semester after semester, year after year—until it was hard for me to tell whether I was helping Ken with his writing or whether Ken was helping me with my teaching. Who knows, maybe the two were the same thing.

SUSAN O'CONNOR wouldn't mind my telling the story of how Ken once took her up to Grand Central Station after the NYU writing class, and because Susan was a little overwhelmed by the challenge of her own writing and her own life and because she seemed to need someone she could talk to about it, Ken got on her train to Greenwich, Connecticut, and he stayed on that train with her until it reached Stamford, where he got off and got on a return train to New York. What is important about this story is that Ken wasn't on the make for Susan, he was simply exercising the very highest kind of chivalry.

I MENTION how the 1960's were years of tremendous turmoil and social protest, and how Ken McLaren was involved in a very great deal of it. We lived nearby so we'd often meet each other on 14th Street outside Max Siegel's SNAP CAMERA and Ken would always have some latest instance of outrage against the body politic. I'd stand and listen patiently as Ken went on and on and on, and sometimes I'd interrupt and say I didn't think anyone could right the wrongs of our silly civilization because things had simply gone too far. And Ken would listen to me and then he would chuckle amiably. But I knew damn well that no matter what I might say to him, Ken would keep right on being Ken, and thank god for that, because he helped an awful lot of other individuals get in touch with their own inner awareness.

Then I read a poem I wrote for Ken way back in September 1966:

ON HEARING KEN McLAREN

> *you are*
> *a reporter*
> *of sorts*
>
> *whose most*
> *important*
> *stories*
>
> *are often*
> *off–color*
> *odes*
>
> *to the happy*
> *sadness of*
> *being bad*
>
> *O bard of birds*
> *and broads and*
> *butterflies*
>
> *you specialize*
> *in ways of*
> *saying yes*

*yet you are
also wise to
what goes on*

*behind the
eyes, inside
the mind*

*with sideways
sight you spy
out the disguise*

*express it in
a free form
laughter*

*O poet's poet
you go on
composing*

*ping pong
poems which
expose*

*all those
who have
a genius*

*for being
inexcusably
unpleasant*

I SIT DOWN, the memorial service is over, and the organ begins
playing the great Martin Luther protestant hymn *A MIGHTY
FORTRESS IS OUR GOD,* and these two lines stay in my mind:

    *let goods and kindred go
this mortal life also. . .*

*   *   *

A HALF YEAR LATER, Donald Lev's *HOME PLANET NEWS*
publishes a memorial to Ken McLaren that is written by RobertOh
Faber, in Volume 1 #5, January 1980. And this is what RobertOh
Faber has to say about Ken:

*This past summer, Ken McLaren, a veteran of New York's
poetry scene, died of a cerebral hemorrhage in his apartment.
He was 63. The news came as a shock. Ken was someone
I had thought of as "perennial." I expected him to go on
forever calling me up in the middle of the night.*

*Ken McLaren was a man of many parts, many reincarnations
within his own lifetime. Most readers will remember him
best as a poet, one of the original Ganesvoort Pier people,
others most for his strong involvement in civil- and human-
rights activities.*

*Still others knew him as a proprietor of "Ken McLaren's
Sechoir," a men's fashion store on Greenwich Avenue. There
was nothing dry about Sechoir. The police issued Ken a
summons for having the sidewalk in front of the store painted
in broad stripes, reaching to the curb, of hot Mediterranean
colors. It was one of the first stores to carry unusual clothing
and accessories such as ethnic imports. Ken also ran an invest-
ment business for a while (just by way of illustrating his varied
career).*

*Others remember him as an almost compulsive photographer,
a camp follower of the performances of Julian Beck and Judith
Malina's Living Theatre, of which he took scores of magnificent,
extremely dramatic photographs.*

*I remember when Radio Station WNYC refused to allow broad-
cast of a poem Ken had already taped for its Open Poetry pro-
gram. The poem was a reaction to the deliberate and unlawful
beating of dissenters (and innocent bystanders) by police in
Chicago in 1968. The poem contains none of what are conven-
tionally regarded as obscenities; it simply repeated various
epithets used by the police during these vicious beatings of
people whose politics or nationality they did not like. It was
in vain pointed out to the station's Program Manager that the
poem was **disapproving** of police use of these epithets, that
that disapproval was what the poem was **about**. The station,
in a flurry of irrational obtuseness, accused Ken McLaren (of
all people!) of being "a bigot" and "against minorities" and of
"using obscene words." Ken said, "I expected to make the
bigot's lists, not WNYC's." Supporters picketed the station with
denunciatory placards. Later the poem became the basis of a
sketch performed at the Village Vanguard. Here's the poem:*

*(This is dedicated to the kids, the hippies and yippies,
Abbie Hoffman, Jerry Rubin, Paul Krasner, and Bob
Fass, Ed Sanders, Tuli Kupferberg and Ken Weaver—
and particularly dedicated to the Fugs, who have gone
on to Prague, from Chicago, to confront the same old
Law and Order.)*

BANNED BY STATION WNYC IN NEW YORK

LEG AND BOOT OF THE LAW

*Individual policemen / want to beat people / who they believe are /
"not our kind" / unamerican / dirty / disrespectful.*

(nervous nellies)
(commies)
(young nomads)
(photographers)
(protesters)
(students)
(international plotters)
(trouble-makers)
(resistance fighters)
(drunks)
(foul mouths)
(smart alecs)
(beatniks)
(left-wingers)
(radicals)
(reliefers)
(low-lifes)
(pornographers)
(dirty old men)
(sex fiends)
(dirty old women)
(seducers)
(Lolitas)
(baby studs)
(immorals)
(welfare people)
(unwed mothers)
(dirty-mouths)
(bums)
(unchristians)
(hippies)
(yippies)
(intellectuals)
(reporters)
(TV cameramen)
(theorists)
(riff raff)
(micks)
(hunkies)
(polacks)
(bleeding hearts)
(wops)
(krauts)
(frogs)
(potheads)
(disloyals)
(pinkos)

(dope addicts)
(peaceniks)
(vietniks)
(long hairs)
(minority creeps)
(black apologists)
(black deacons)
(defenders)
(black power bastards)
(black panthers)
(non-violent objectors)
(war resisters)
(cop–haters)
(perverts) (preverts)
(social workers)
(ministers)
(priests)
(rabbis)
(humanists)
(half-breeds)
(wetbacks)
(slant-eyes)
(indian creeps)
(freaks)
(cowards)
(anarchists)
(nonconformists)
(irresponsibles)
(unreliables)
(immatures)
(marxists)
(queers)
(heterosexuals)
(niggers)
(spics)
(kikes)
(the unwashed)
(traitors)
(desecrators)
(draft dodgers)
(beady people)
(flower children)
(poets)
(freedom fighters)
(scum)
(whores)
(pimps)
(do-gooders)
(beards)
(bare feet)
(etc. etc. and)
(etceteras)

*Without the courageous Americanism / of our local police /
who would stop / these evil people?*

DMZ at the Village Vanguard
by Jerry Tallmer

The DMZ, founded last year on upper Broadway by Eric Bentley and Isaiah Sheffer—Columbia professors, men of theater, nonconservatives—was an attempt at a political cabaret in the pre-Hitler Berlin style, something this city has long needed and sometimes tried for, never with complete success. The group that called itself The Premise perhaps came closest.

By now, you get the idea. So did Max Gordon, proprietor of the Village Vanguard since history began. At intermission the night I went he found himself remembering The Revuers, circa 1939—Judy Holiday, Adolph Green, Betty Comden & Co.

The material, songs and skits, is by people ranging from Jacques Prevert to Jules Feiffer as well as the two theater-minded professors, and there are four performers whose gifts grow on you as the evening advances: James Antonio, Cynthia Harris, Morgan Freeman, Jon Bauman; the latter, a very recent Columbia graduate, serving also as pianist.

Good Poem

There is, perhaps best of all, a sketch on the cops by Ken McLaren, consisting mostly of a rapid-fire incredibly long list of people the police do not cotton to.

N Y Post, Monday, October 14, 1968

A relative of Ken's once pityingly described him to me as "brain-damaged." He certainly had a different kind of brain/mind, and his own way of seeing and being in the world. One could wish one's brain were damaged in a similar way. His lifelong pursuit of the "higher consciousness," whatever that might turn out to be, was part and parcel of his activist concerns. He was above all a multi-dimensional human being.

Ken's poems are full of life and wonder and human concern and affirmation and love.

—RobertOh Faber

*   *   *

NOW HERE IT IS almost two years after Ken's death and we are just getting around to putting together this small collection of his poems. Over this past year I had a lot of conversations with Ken in the back of my mind, telling him I would get around to doing this book as soon as I got myself out from under the latest workload of debt and drudgery I had inherited. And always in the back of my mind I would hear Ken's amiable chuckle: "It's all right, doctor, don't go getting yourself all exercised about it."

I THINK KEN would be genuinely moved if he knew how many people loved and admired him and his work. Here is a random sampling of comments from some of our outstanding contemporary poets and playwrights and writers and people, about Ken McLaren and his work:

To me, you are a black poet.
LANGSTON HUGHES

His words are made to be seen and sung. He is to our future what Allen Ginsberg has been to our present.
THE LIVING THEATRE COLLECTIVE

You are one with the wonder ones.
ED SANDERS

Ken McLaren, who was always writing while I was talking, would have enjoyed this, me writing one of the forewords to his book. I often think, "Ken would have enjoyed this." About many things. Ken's enjoyments were many—writing, drawing, posing, photo- graphing, eating, reading, listening, talking, posturing, leafletting, buttoning, button-holing, cheering, lightening, rhyming, not rhyming, elevating, levitating, calling, answering, foot stomping, living, loving, and turning people around. Ken really loved to turn people around and make them feel good about themselves. Sometimes when I find myself enjoying something and thinking, "Ken would enjoy that," I feel that Ken is alive. I feel like calling him and telling him about it. If there is enjoyment after life, Ken is laughing somewhere and turning people around.
BOB FASS

You must write a novel, a biography, and more.
ANAIS NIN

You compress a full novel in a single page. Don't stop.
MARGUERITE YOUNG

Peace Joy Love Eternity.
STEVE BEN ISRAEL

Pleasure with humanity and glowing love permeates his work. He must be published, expanded and enjoyed.
JUDITH MALINA

Ken is great fun. We want more from him.
IZZY YOUNG

Ken lets me know I am alive and he encourages me to be glad I am.
PAUL KRASNER

*Ken McLaren knows he is good. He does **not** know how good he really is. The word genius and the consciousness of Gurdjieff come first to my mind. He is the only man I know who has G's consciousness.*
LINCOLN KIRSTEIN

Ken McLaren's whole life was a poem he kept jotting down in journals, on napkins in restaurants, on scraps of paper, etc., and he carried it with him in his bundle of brown paper bags. It took his dying to "fix" the poems on pages to form the book of his poems. The blues is Ken not around to read his poems any more.
SUSAN O'CONNOR

Ken McLaren's poems give us all courage to sustain our own efforts. They come from that part of the heart that works even if emotions go and the only thing a poet has is what he leaves us. These poems are moving, compassionate, disturb where they should.
LEO CONNELLAN

Ken McLaren confers that special insight of the unexpected and he is devoted to the cause of the underdog.
MARJORIE FINNELL

*   *   *

WHAT MORE can one say? I have two copies of statements that I wrote for Ken, one in 1970, the other one undated. These were the sort of "official" letters that one writes when someone else is applying for a grant and needs formal-type letters of recommendation. I write lots of letters like this for lots of people and usually I crank out lots of meaningless generalities saying what a fine fellow so & so is, etc. But I can remember when I wrote these two letters for Ken McLaren, I meant every word of what I was saying. Here are the letters:

June 14, 1970

TO WHOM IT MAY CONCERN:

I have known Ken McLaren as student, as poet, and as friend, for almost eight years now, and the admiration I had for his work has grown into a warm awe at what he has achieved in his work and in his life.

He is that extraordinary and rare combination, an authentic poet and a concerned human being. His poems convey the sharp insight he has into the world around him, in such a way as to inspire change, or at least rage and compassion . . .

.   .   .

TO WHOM IT MAY CONCERN:

Ken is an active, caring, and creative member of the community of people who are working to make this a better world. He has given unsparingly of his own time and energy towards the welfare of others, and he has written some outstanding poetry in pursuit of his own objective as artist and creative human being.

Ken has had an important impact on the lives of many people, and for that reason alone, I think he is deserving of support for his work. . .

*   *   *

FOR THE RECORD, as they say, here is a brief biography of Ken McLaren:

HE WAS BORN January 13, 1917, in Berkeley, California. He went to primary schools in Berkeley, and the Thatcher School in Ojai, California. He spent one year in France and Germany with his grandfather in 1936-1937, where he had a chance to see firsthand the menace of mass mind as it was steamrollering towards total cataclysm in Europe. He came back to attend college at the University of California at Berkeley, where he belonged to Psi Upsilon fraternity. At the age of 17 he was editing a Tahoe newspaper, and at the University he put out his own newsletter and he also got involved with the One World movement and he also created his own Ken McLaren chocolate bar.

HE MOVED to New York City at the end of 1944, and those first years in New York were a terrific exaltation of self-discovery, but they were also periods of profound pain and self-doubt. He spent some time in the Tombs. He once wrote a letter to the *EAST VILLAGE OTHER* outlining a bitter money dispute he had had with his family. He hit the bottle pretty heavily, so that it became necessary for him to get deeply involved with the ongoing activities of Alcoholics Anonymous. He worked in Mutual Funds, and he was in and out of the management of two separate men's shops.

DURING THESE YEARS in New York, Ken created his own self-portrait in a series of statements that he wrote for various poetry readings and arts organizations. These statements say it all. They show Ken McLaren's easy-going insouciant friendly madcap witty sane equanimity. Here are the statements:

> *1968: poetry today is indeed bread and potatoes to the younger generation, and not only an occasional pink birthday cake. . .*

> *1970: I am an original Yippie, supporting the Panthers (black and white), Chicanos, Young Lords, and I am Order of LaFayette (queen of England) and Society of Cincinnatus (the top U.S. society). . .*

> *1971: almost every day I try to deal with cases of the aging men without hope who are only waiting to die. Many of them have only enough money to send out for one or two sandwiches a day and spend almost all their time in the remaining flophouses on the Bowery.*

> *(undated): I am called a poet and I am supposed to present you some acceptable examples of the art, in this case mine. So I should warn you: I am not impressed by any art spelt with a capital A! Rather I agree with Lao Tsu that the way to do is be! Sure, it's fine to form a nice rhyme, perhaps with a witty intellectual laugh. But that's not my goal. I am writing for you something that must communi-cate or it isn't great to me. I like a poem to evoke your hooray, not as successful exercise, not as recognizable art, rather as something that speaks from my heart to yours. What is a poem? No one is authorized by God to say what's not! That is as far as definition sensibly goes.*

*Art is a rose or a loved one's toes, a kaleidoscope or a line encouraging
hope or art is a joke. Art is the Blues or a luscious cake. But art isn't
rape of body or heart. Art is escape or facing up. But the poet (there
are no poetesses!) is a person who allows words or images or some-
thing at least (!) to say what often surprises the poet. I am called a
poet. If you don't get something out of my play with words and
stuff I am not living up to what I wish to be. Do my words tell you
you contain something great you may not have learned to truly
appreciate? Do I bring tears of appreciative self-recognition to YOUR
eyes? Are there cries of hope, understanding, empathy, surprise? If so,
both of us know it was worth the many million tries! Clever verse is
often lies and works of art are often mysteries to me. But something
reaching you does something for me that makes me feel wonderful to be.*

*   *   *

WELL HERE YOU ARE, KEN. This is the book of poems that you were writing
over a period of some 40-odd years. I've tried to choose carefully from the cartons
and cartons of loose papers that are still sitting in the other room of my apartment.
At their best, your poems breathe with the immediacy of Li Po, the careless passion
of Catullus, the insouciance of Issa, and the mischievous wit of E.E. Cummings. It's
all there in an instant of air, which is where you are right now, Ken, chuckling
amiably as I am trying to write these lines for you.

William Packard
New York City

HELLO, KEN, WE NEVER MET

It's raining soft rain, Ken, on this sad afternoon of your death discovery. The last time I saw you I was a child. I stand in your village basement apartment of thirty years and although you're gone I can still feel your magic here. The uncle I never had. I reach towards you: black lace clouds covering a bright full moon. **NOBODY FOR PRESIDENT** *poster on your wall and your photos of the classic New York City architecture and everywhere shopping bags—there must be hundreds here, and all the dust, Ken—it's like velvet lying on your poems. Your writings piled high just waiting to be gone through and published. Your wonderful words you slyly captured. You wrote:*

> **"Look, Ma, no hands! Words are
> driving me! I am a cabdriver with
> words for passengers!....Ma! Words
> smiled at me!"**

Thirty years of possessions piled high on every surface— your last thirty years and my first thirty. Your friends told me you never lost your sense of humor and never held a grudge and our middle names are the same. The uncle I never had—you left us all your treasures and trash to go through, so much filth and magic just like this city. I dream you whole through your voice on tape, photographs of you and your poems and drawings here before me. The layers, Ken, the layers of your life. I grab your journal open on your bed with left-handed square printing like mine, and step out into the rain—I want to run and scream, but I stand looking at your words and they begin to run down the page. I think of new flowers as you and the curves of the Chrysler building.

Hello, Ken, goodbye from your niece, Annie Mac.

YES
WITH VARIATIONS

Yes
with variations
is affirmation
concerning the full range of yes
from absolutely **yes**
to **damn it! no**
with an infinitude of yeses
in between
including
why should I?
you don't think I (actually!) would?
and
do you think I'm crazy?
I'd do *this* **for that?**
and more variations than
a volume
expanded
to the **yes** *power of* **yes**
could ever contain

Yes
with variations
is saying yes *to life*
variously
as life itself is
(variously)
saying **yes** *to you*
and it is more the recognition
that many a firm **no**
is (truly) a giving-full **yes**
than it is a catalog of
surprise
with **yes**
with variations
life is being
accepted
appreciated
enjoyed
encouraged
and it is
(furthermore!)
more fun.

YES WITH VARIATIONS

YES is bacon in the mountains.

YES is making up your mind to be happy, and then behaving as if you believe yourself.

YES is when somebody else confesses.

YES is finding how much fun it is to know that you can still wiggle your big toe when they told you to be completely still.

YES is when she calls you when she said she would.

YES is a ride on the Staten Island Ferry.

YES is a rabbit finding another rabbit.

YES is discovering there is a new book just published, in your favorite bookstore, by your favorite poet, and you're passing the bookstore and you have the price of the book in your pocket, and you discover that your feet are headed IN.

YES is why the scrawny little man who knew what he wanted won the big beautiful blonde who couldn't make up her mind.

YES is coming home late to discover there isn't a single squeaky board in the hall.

YES is going home early with a book for the first time and beginning the book, discovering that what so many of your friends found you also were finding in *LEAVES OF GRASS.*

YES is believing what Jesus said.

YES is believing what Socrates said.

YES is believing what Buddha said.

YES is believing what Moses said.

YES is believing what Whitman said.

YES is believing what e.e. cummings said.

YES is believing what Spinoza said.

YES is saying what you believe.

YES is other people believing what you say.

YES is other people believing what you believe.

YES is believing in the essential goodness of man.

(And believing in the essential goodness of yourself.)

YES is the blank check written out to me by the Universe.

NO is believing you have to please someone else.

YES is discovering that what really matters is how you react to what happens.

YES is all the things that have ever happened to me after I decided they would.

YES is why I'm writing now, for I no longer feel I need hesitate when I have a clear desire.

YES is a big tail, wagging a little dog, because you are home.

YES is why Lucy goes away.

YES is being so excited about a new project you wake up early.

FREEDOM is discovering she is already married.

HUMOR is someone else slipping on a banana peel.

LIFE is awareness.

FUN is when you want to go somewhere very much and you already have tickets.

FREEDOM is getting there (on your own) in spite of helpful people.

POETRY is higher levels of emotion or meaning, or both, carrying glimpses of words synergistically into minds and onto paper where they live as a new entity.

FREEDOM is not so much what you do as what you know you can do.

FREEDOM is dancing a jig.

FREEDOM is having fifty dollars more than you thought you had in your bank account.

FREEDOM is realizing the worst that could happen doesn't matter that much.

FREEDOM is when they take the cast off.

YES is the entire vocabulary of the still, small voice inside of me.

NOTHING is merely a *NO* with nowhere to go.

WE are consciousness using body, never body using consciousness.

FREEDOM is monkeys, monkeying around.

AMERICA is invention, destination, circulation.

AMERICA is more people from more places getting along better than they ever had before (which still means a lot of fighting).

AMERICA is where you bawl out your President, but usually sign your letter *"Respectfully."*

AMERICA is love poetry being written by more lonely people than seems likely.

AMERICA is 100,000,000 slightly out of focus television sets, a billion books, and more artificial sweetener than most countries have sugar.

WRITER is a person who can't not write.

NOW is all the life you can possibly know.

FREEDOM is looking deep in her eyes, happy you married her.

FREEDOM is children's laughter when it doesn't have to stop.

LOVE is giving the other person your hearing aid, your money, and your wife.

FREEDOM is a blonde who wants to be blonde more than anything else.

LOVE is why I believe you when I know you are lying.

TYRANNY is being represented when you do not wish to be represented.

TYRANNY is being misrepresented.

JAZZ is sound that sends you, not the volume of the sound.

MATERIALISM is the indestructibly describable.

NOT is when you see her, nothing else is urgent.

DEBT is a mean old buzzard word.

PUPPY is a playful son of a bitch.

GRAVEYARD is the final resting place for what no longer needs a rest.

PEACE is when both of you trust the referee.

AMERICA is poets, poetry, and (occasionally) a poem.

FREEDOM is one person saying *NO* when all the rest are nodding *YES.*

FREEDOM is my right to go to sleep in the church of my own choice.

FREEDOM is thinking about freedom on a full stomach.

FREEDOM is accepting the fact there are some things I cannot accept.

FREEDOM is a loose thought and a tight dress.

MOTHER is to have a baby; FATHER is to wish it were his; CHILD is to wonder why.

SEXY is *don't blame me if I make a grab for you, you asked for it, (or nature did it for you!) and baby, you got something really going for you!*

FREEDOM is having a gun so fast I may never have to use it.

POEM is a rocket in consciousness, breaking through time, space, and (the all-too-human) condition.

FREEDOM is daisies conquering fences.

FREEDOM is rabbits confounding the census.

DREAM is the iceberg part of mind, working something out while the surface mind rests.

SINNER is a man who does it right out in the open.

SILENCE is what you don't hear when you don't listen.

YOUTH is an imperfection much coveted by the old.

EXPERIENCE is what you say you accumulate when you don't succeed in accumulating money.

HAPPINESS is your aunt's unbelievable gift arriving smashed beyond any recognition.

HAPPINESS is a most independent cat, choosing your leg to rub against.

BIG BOY is little boy who hated girls now grown much more tolerant.

LONELINESS is a tall wall, tremendously tall, with you crying small beneath it.

LONELINESS is when who it is that really matters is not there.

FREEDOM is spotting your own neurosis so you can prevent it from really bopping you.

FREEDOM is looking in the mirror and not wanting to hit what you see.

FUN is a beautiful girl going home with you.

FREEDOM is deciding to do it!

GHETTO is wherever too many people live, by fact of entrapment rather than by choice.

GHETTO is a huge pay toilet where the people are trapped and must pay over and over and over again just to keep from being drowned.

BLACK is the end result of inter-appreciation of many peoples.

TAO is 360° awareness, with the visible and invisible as one.

TIME is JESUS saying "Before Abraham was, I AM."

FREEDOM is sending her a dozen red roses when neither of us expects it.

PEOPLE ARE BEAUTIFUL
IN THE MORNING

People are beautiful
in the morning
when they are sure
they are at their most
untogether
ungathered as to thoughts
and poise
uneasy though well groomed
un up to handling themselves
(and others like them)

They have troubled expressions
on serene faces
They have the cares of their world
on virgin shoulders

People are beautiful
in the morning
(especially)
before they discover
each other again,
before they find out.

LIKE

The way I like people
is
they take you
      the way you are
whether they know
      the way you are
or not.

Here I am
peeing
at almost the speed of sound
37,000 feet in the air
pressurized in this cabin
yet steady   easy
cool   me neatly
as if man were made for
this (occasionally bumpy) life
shot through upper air
casually   naturally
and sensationally
anywhere.

NAKED UNIQUE

*Sometimes when you bite into
something,
and your tongue rolls over it,
as a perfect peach,
sensation is so tongue–right
it is as if another act were
being performed,
greater and more shaking
and it is a different
dimension.*

*Just so
the look of you,
so very don't-ever-leave-me
(already),
is greater
in a way that would be
even more wonderful
for trying;
eyes, fingers, lips,
to measure
this texture,
this ecstasy of touch
that is so very you.*

UNSETTLED MUSCLES

He is matter of fact affectionate,
and big pussy-cat soft
with a potential for mammoth maneuvers.
His muscles
seem to have settled
in some sort of
super-satisfactory arrangement
that makes strong men
envious
and weak women
feel strong enough
for (at least!) a little while.
It would be marvelous
to look in the mirror
some great day
and see him looking back
at you,
even over your shoulder.

BLOODY WAR WHOOP OF THE FBI

(TO PREVENT SIOUX PEACE SUBVERSION)

(April 14, 1967—NY)

You goddamned unamerican indians gotta keep
your disloyal bodies
outa here
we won't let you non-citizens
mobilize
for peace
the fbi
won't let you leave the dakotas
shit on you all over all over again
on all one hundred of you
which is the nasty reminder
we failed of a final
100% american
solution
to the enemy minority problem
as hitler failed to kill all jews everywhere
we john wayne marine corps unamerican activities americans
failed
to shoot stab poison burn gas bury drown
      all the viets
      all the sioux
      all the beats
      all the poets
      all the peace creeps
      all the hippies
      all the love people
      all the flower children
      all the members of
      all the tribes

the usa is in peril
the indians are loose
again
the fbi is holding back the american alien tide
patriotically restraining
(harassing)
many of the one hundred
goddamned unamerican indians
to keep their disloyal bodies
outa here
we in the new york   american flag-wavers' melting pot say
stay away from here you red creeps
you may incite us to riot you dead
except for a few of you
obedient relics
uncle tom-toms
oddities
who reassure us
who are stuck in guarded cages
picturesquely
called reservations
where faded war whoops are only a tourist sound effect
for the protection and amusement of 100% red white and blue
true loyal patriotic americans
who come to marvel at what
the cia fbi etc
have saved them
from.

RIGHT (UNPASSING) NOW

Before Abraham or Jesus was
I am (very much am)
(with them I am)
with all these great/this I am
Then is when
my living time is
I am living then
and now
in indivisibility
Not passing time I am
I am living time
That which I am endures
as consciousness
Not as hope
nor as a guess
I am that I am
before and during
and to be
relaxed I am
in my unpassing now
(right now)

NOT ALL

"You talk to them—
they're all *your* friends*"*

(negroes)
(egyptians)
(greeks)
(red indians)
(yellow indians)
(black spanish)
(jewish merchants)
(garbage men)
(homesick marines)
(homosexuals)
(he-men)
(she-women)
(conservatives)
(neurotics)
(actresses)
(drunken housewives)
(other women)
(drag queens)
(fortune tellers)
(lesbians)
(millionaires)
(unwashed scotsmen)
(poets)
(policemen)
(topless waitresses)
(uncircumcised irish)
(liberals)
(italians)
(genial prostitutes)
(priests)

"Listen, Mac—not all of **anything**
is my friends."

INSIDE THEIR LOONY WARD

I have lived among the mad / deranged / senile /
sad / and the estranged / those who withdraw
to their paranoid interiors
to nightmare landscapes
burnt within their minds
I have seen their darting / seeking eyes
I have heard their anguish cries
I have smelt their fright
understood their dangers / often real /
amongst the rubbage of their frantic lives
I have tasted the bitterness
the terror of their tears
and we have touched / communions
of the damned
I have known their unreal retreats
and occasional regression
I have burst with that agony
and yet
I have taken part
in the return of some to the "more real"
been present on their journey
to a marvelous recovery
inside their loony ward
and on the street.

Betty Reading The Latest Betty Poem

sighed

and sighing again

Sometimes, she said with a sigh

I wish

this Betty broad

were me.

THE BIRDS ARE BACK

And they are hardly cooling it
Like now
As soon as they arrive
Another noisy
All-talk-at-once convention
Outside our place
Cheep Cheep Cheep —
That's times a hundred! —
All over our skies
Over trees
Over yards
Birds and their nutty calls
Out-shout
Our brightest drapes
And the scarlet orange flaming
Potted plants
Full in our windows
The birds blot out all living things
From view
With their blatant
Joyousness
Cheep Cheep Cheep —
Make that times a million! —
I swear it is as if
They'd never go,
Nor have they been,
Away.
They holler
Laugh and interrupt
All over the place.
It seems natural
To hear them.
THE BIRDS ARE BACK
And so damn cheerful
I'm glad they make
This scene!

ALL OF IT

Is there such a thing as
retrosexual?
I hope so.
I feel I must
(I absolutely must!)
go back
and do it
(all of it)
again and again and
again
with you.

OVER MY OWN HEAD

On the pier of many poets
I read over my head
this afternoon
It must have been
the touch of sinus
or the antihistamine
in the cold tablets
that made me a
little less alert
than usual
and my poetry
did not seem
as interesting to me
as at other times
Perhaps it was
because I could not
understand it very well
Let's face it
Being dopey
(sometimes)
I really write
quite over
my own
head

HAPPY THERAPY!

I am a
(firm)
believer in
therapeutic
mass-
intercourse
for
in order to
let no one
feel
left out
it may
(very well!)
be necessary to
indulge in a
great multiplicity of
togetherness
and to (physically)
admit
we all do
(indeed)
love
love
love
one another—
and so forth!

APPLES EVERY DAY

If boys were apples
she would like to go
bobbing
almost more than anything
and she would
go to great lengths
(psychologically)
to make out like
it was everyday
Hallowe'en!

WINTERSCAPE

Though the swimming pool is filled with snow
and the cesspool digger's sign across the way
aims its arrow at the pool I know
it does not interrupt our winterscape
double-tonguing talk of peace–sad woe
like hearing sirens scream their fearful: *go!*
We know we'll stay. We know there's no escape.
We're in man's sad and transient winterscape.
We waiting know we may disintegrate.

Belly warming belly
in turn warmed
by other belly
holding firm against receptive flesh
while up above
breath is meeting breath
(as if double bellows)
mirror blew
thus does each
the other know
and in knowing
is each one
growing
ever
warmer!

MARGUERITE, I SOUND YOUR NAME

Marguerite, I sound your name.
Your death to me is now less real,
for alive in me is remembrance
of the fascination in people
(preference over things)
the small insignificant observation
that often tells the all.

I sound your name, Marguerite,
and hear your doubts of me
expressed
when you could have yessed my negatives,
my self-righteous sober nastiness.

I sound your name, Marguerite,
and hear you say,
why not be pleasant, relaxed?
Why not go along with it
and not just fight this day?
And I know what I never knew then.

I sound your name, Marguerite,
and know that then
to sound your name
was to utter wonder—
How long could you last?
Would it be by wreck,
by stroke, or by worse?

Now that death's time is past,
death receded and
is less real
and you are (once more)
real in my remembrance.
The many (human) faults,
and the many affirmations, Marguerite,
these are you in memory.

You are your preference
for persons over things,
for the lesser traits of lesser people,
(and the same for mammoth men)
for tiny quirks and for
throw-away gestures.

I sound your name, Marguerite,
and you come up alive, come up right
more than I knew you knew,
the very human that you knew
(when you were here for the knowing)
when I missed your lesson,
when I saw your death
breathing down both our necks,
I did not see you,
Marguerite.

Her name was Jean/and we shared another miracle/that day when we skidded/
safely to her drive/and she dismounted/laughing/pink and flushed/
and merry in the midst/of her golden swirls of hair/and I/
(who felt I was learning all about girls)/planned to park my bike/
and follow her/but she said no!/and I must not!/because people might not
understand.

She said her sister might get angry/and her mother/and her brother/
and thank you (she said)/it was a lovely ride/and we ought to get together/
(vaguely)/some other time/and goodbye for now/and my face felt hot/
(and my ears stung)/and I wanted to hide/afraid of what/all the kids/
and all the merchants/all the other prying eyes/we had just wind and wonder passed/
would think.

Wouldn't they all know/(surely)/we had parted/just like that?/
so I drove away/crazy away/fast/and far/drove away *away*/
and more out of the way for me/and wore out/all my energies/
rode up and down strange blocks/and strange looks/from strangers/
(which didn't matter)/and I didn't come back/to where I knew people/
until I thought/the (obvious) shame/was gone/when they wouldn't know.

Her name was Jean/and she and I/never shared the wind again/
together.

SOME OTHER TIME

Carry me back to
old Nantucket
and do all the
things
that rhyme

Fry me
some
from old Virginny
so I can have me a
piece
and have me a time

And save me
nice slices
(and some
rhymeable things)

And I'll have me
some more stuff
some other time

I'll find me a piece
and I'll find me a bucket
and I'll learn
how to rhyme.

"HEY, I *LIKE* YOUR FISH"

"Hey, I *like* your fish,"
she said to him
as he came out of the shower
with it,
the bronze
loose–tail,
very shiny
fish.
"How like a lure,"
she cried.
"How I like your
lure,"
she giggled.
"My!
how it wiggles
and catches my eye."
He stopped in
full stride as her
"Hey, I *like* your fish"
was more muffled
and the lure
lost its shine,
lost its wiggle.

IT IS TIRED AND I AM LATE

I think
I'll have
a love
affair
before
I go
to bed,

but if
at first
I look
at you,
I may go
straight
to bed
instead.

22 WORDS WITH BIRDS

Some people think
the birds
ought to apologize
to god
for their biology
as if they
and he
weren't doing it
together.

Q & A

What is it like
(I have so often
        wondered)
going to bed
with a man
with a long
pointed
beard?
My dear, it is like
going to bed
with a friendly
goat.

IT IS MY PROUD GUILT
AND I AM ACTIVITIES

(To the memory of
Brecht's appearance
before the House
Committee on Un-
american Activities
in 1949)

I don't care what
they accuse me of
I feel I am guilty
of everything
and that which I can't
claim guilt for
that which I haven't thought of
yet
that which I haven't encountered
yet
include it all

I would take it
as a great compliment
if you would
(at least)
believe me
guilty.

TO WHOM IT MAY CONCERN:
I'M ACCIDENT PRONE!

Sex
is a deliberate
accident
from blushing first stammers to
wordless blush of clitoris
each and every thing lands
right side down and up
in the right places
in the right time
in the right way
with the right result
and then
the words gush forth once more
and out pours the lament:
it was an
accident! —
Until
the next
intent.

KING OF THE MAY
for Allen Ginsberg

We hail thee: King of the May!
So gay it cannot for more than
A month
(For many for more than a day
It cannot)
We hail thee: detained May King
May saluter of youth
Bearded symbol of virile
Expending!
Unending!
Except for the final descending
Of May.

You, Now

the salt of your tits
the sweet of your thighs
the *no* on your lips
and the *yes* in your eyes
make yesterday nothing but lies

Love is a true friend, or
We've met someplace, I swear

Everyone is better off
Than someone.

I knew
There must be
One
Good reason for
Knowing you.

LIVING THEATRE

People were there
melting into one another
soft and warm
and it was flesh all the way
through his flesh
and his *other* flesh
which was *her* flesh sometimes
and another *his's* flesh
some other times

And it was real / firm / throb
warm / cool / damp
marble / marbled / nobbed
hard real *all* of the time

It sucked touch
all the way up
its mind's vaginas

patting softly baby shapes
and planning later lovely babies
while it was there
taking loving hold
of mother's mold

People melting into
each other's flesh
not mesh now
and not marble now
and not mix
and not superimpose
not boil / not froze
it was flesh in *one* place
all at once
so it *rose* and fell
short hot fast
live *movement*
all the time

until the two
or three or four
were *one*.

HIS OUT OF FACE

He grew so old his face fell off
and artichokes filled out his fallen cheek
with leaves of leftover sad

He grew too old to greet each day
Steps though slow and smooth
fell from him in strange stone unopen ways

Once when his moustache was pasted back on
the look it was meant for
was too far gone
to be put on with it
so it too had to be dropped

When his too stone oldness
and his fallen off him face
drag up our swollen street
not even beggars seem to be
aware of him

So stone old no flowers open up for him
since they have found only disappointments
when they came out before

His steps no longer stagger past
no now none of him
abandoned doors on by
none of him
that is
except a stumbled memory
of his alienated moustache
and his out of face
stone fallen
stare.

I SEE THE YOUNG POET

I see the young poet frown,
I will never amount to anything.
I pour everything I can summon up
Into one or two lines a day,
And they do not seem good enough
To me.

Young poet,
You so lyric,
(For I have read your lines
And I salute you),
I see you standing straight
In confidence
In honest pride.

You will learn to be glad
Of your poetry
Some day,
That your lines do sing.

THE MISSION IN THE TRIP

*I saw inside the head of each person I passed /
on sidewalk and street / I saw sad circumstance
and agony / I saw confusion doubt and love / I
saw joy and pride / I saw fear / I saw bravery /
I saw hunger / I saw the sad / the lost / the
good / I saw goodness everywhere / I went past
empathy to tears / I could have cried with each
of the lost / and I could have cried with those
filled with pleasure / friendship / peace /
and happiness / No one's mind or heart could
remain hidden from my X-ray vision / It grew to
be too much for me / I found myself averting
their eyes / their faces / even their bodies /
I struggled onward to a mysterious destiny /
filled with a missionary fervor / Movement was
difficult*

*It started at home / this feeling something had
to be done for my fellow humans / I was so high
I had to peel my body from the ceiling / before
I could get ready to make my move / and then I
knew only that I had to get to upper midtown /
The time was past three a.m. / When I hit the
topsy-turvy outside world / roller-coaster
sidewalks caught me / in a contagion of gyration /
They repeatedly rose with the lift of a rocket /
and fell with the drop of a lost elevator / My
stomach kept meeting itself going up and coming
back down / My vision flashed frightening images /
in the midst of the grinding blur in my head /
Neither sight nor insight was able to tell me /
what was happening / or where / or who / I was*

*The judgement room / etched in my mind by a
massive multiple dose of acid / thirty trips or
more / polluted by speed / and other agents all
at once / the judgement room flashed on and off
in my consciousness / and I heard again and again
the questions of the judges / and my answers /
and I heard her voice / and I knew it was starting
to happen*

*As I maneuvered the rolling streets / often in the
middle / I managed to move across town / and then
uptown / And the big plan began to construct itself
in that upside-down that was my mind / I would keep
my promise to those judges / in eternity / Surely I
would find wide support / support enough / among
my humankind / I would be courageous / I would make
my move / this night / it would be all right /
Nothing but good could come of such a high
motivation*

*Buildings on either side of me rolled as if caught
up by giant shock waves / and cars came and went as if
driven by the wind / Against inopportune forces of
a nature that seemed to have repealed most of its
laws / I found progress a difficult task / and then /
by some inner force I had not suspected before / I
found myself flying / just above the pavements /
higher than the heads of pedestrians / independent
of anyone / although I was powered by pills /
agents of "her" power / round keys to my judgement /
LSD / mescalin / whatever / what came along with
them / I was Mystified by the feeling of invincibility ·*

*I reached midtown and kept going / continuing to fly
up the middle of the street / just above the asphalt /*

*ignoring traffic / cars buses and trucks / seeing
no one / only my nearly resolved objective / Then
I reached a most expensive section / I paused /
looked around / and decided to enter an elegant
bank / It was now close to six a.m. / I walked through
the dimness of early morning / right through the
doors / and through an electronic screen / and then
into an elevator deep inside / No one / caught in the
surprise of my action / had presence of mind to
stop me*

*The guards' mouths had fallen open / Now one spoke /
"How did you get in here?" / Another asked the first /
"How did he get past the security alarm?" / I moved
all the way back in the steel elevator / and there
I refused to budge / "Send me your chief." / I told the
green-clad bank guards / I waited / determined /
knowing what I must do / now really knowing / A
taller security man / neatly uniformed in a conserva-
tively sky-blue uniform / came to the elevator door /
"What is it with you?" / He wanted to know. / "They tell
me you are waiting to speak to me. / I am in charge
here." / "Thank you for coming. / I want you to call
the police for me / I am holding an assortment of
what are called dangerous drugs / I wish to be
arrested." / His surprise and his curiosity had grown. /
"Why do you want to be arrested? / Why don't you just
walk out / quietly / the way you came in / though I
can't figure out how you did it? / Why don't you get
out of here as quickly as you can?" / "I won't go /
not until you get the police to come for me." /
Finally he agreed*

*I stayed inside the steel elevator / quietly waiting /
until the police had arrived / according to his
assurance / I was sure he was telling me the truth /
"The police are waiting for you in front of the
bank. / It is time for you to go." / I followed him
out*

*They were waiting / I was grabbed / and spun
around / pressed against their patrol car / "Put
your arms in the air / and don't move a muscle" /
They searched me / removing several small brown
envelopes from my left jacket pocket / "Is that
all? / All right / Now put your hands behind your
back" / I felt the handcuffs snap shut / They
pinched my wrists a little / It was uncomfortable /
not painful / I had to wiggle trying to get in
the back seat without the use of my hands / One of
them gave me a helpful shove / Then they drove me
to their precinct house / I saw the time on a clock
facing the street / It was six twenty-five / a.m.*

*The trip to the stationhouse was like a boat ride
on deep ocean swells / It felt as logical and
out-of-reality as the LSD and other pills when I had
heard them say to me / (as they might have to Alice!) /
"Take me! Take me! Take me!" / So my great mission
had really begun / My challenge to injustice and
the courts / So there might be no more phoney busts
for reasons of politics / to harrass the young / to
"get" the unfavored minority members of our society /
Kids could go home free / after I succeeded / un-
favored political leaders could walk out of jails /
It would be a better day*

*I was sure I would soon be free / But I couldn't
help wondering / "Was this activist / this fearless
fighter / really me?" / I was much too high to
gravely worry / and I had no urge to try to flee /
It all seemed quite simple / What was really happening
I would find out soon enough.*

TEAR ME UP

*I wrote down
how I loved
you*

*But it didn't
swing
like you*

*I put the poem
back
in my heart*

*I crossed
the paper out—
I tore it up*

*If I look that bad
in ten years
tear me up*

*He must be
kidding
looking like that*

*As if the shirt
and the bourgeois
back of it*

*Were wearing him
and he were wearing
thin*

*Loosely mousey hair
and jellied frame
(heart to match)*

*If the same
were true
of me*

*I'd hope
a stronger
you*

*Would put me
in your heart
alive*

*And cross out
the false words—
and tear me up.*

THE AUTOBIOGRAPHY OF MY DEATH

I am my mother
and she wishes to stay dead,
to stay laid to rest
for the rest of her un—days,
away from the rest of us
who do lie (still ill at ease
on our restless earth)
and do cry
and do contend.

I am all the angers
I ever was
in their full
and fearful turmoil,
without surcease,
not ease in peace
or other agonies,
nor yet down there
beneath earth care
where worms
no longer terrify.

I am he who sees the fully awful
all the time fulfilled,
breathe the noxious air
of care, of stare,
no use—beware
the living held back by limits.

I am my mother who wishes
we would leave her there
past our noxious
too all—assuming air.
Yes, I am my mother
and she wishes to stay laid away
from this and
from all of me.

BLOOD IS RUNNING

The blood is running green alas
My heart pounds firm: bring freedom here
The spilt red blood grows rich green grass

The trillion patriots shout, shall not pass
While tyrant's foot is grinding fear
The blood is running green alas

A million rainbows made of glass
Are in the laughter of one tear
The spilt red blood grows rich green grass

Lessons in freedom not learned in class
Hearts torn open by enslavers' fear
The blood is running green alas

Children's laughter they won't harrass
This right to safety bought so dear
The spilt red blood grows rich green grass

There is more than braying to an ass
Freedom too is more than: cheer!
The blood is running green alas
The spilt red blood grows rich green grass

RECLUSE

Just because they said she burnt her garbage
and didn't flush the toilet
Little mean things they said
The neighbors were reluctant to be seen
talking to old lady Hozier
and she rather welcomed the quiet
private non-interference of this
as she sat on her all-around screened porch
with a worn but working fly-swatter
the latest (March 1, 1928) issue of *Pathfinder*
weekly pulp-paper magazine
neat though overflowing ferns in boy-tall planters
lace curtains and lacier receding memories
of the late devoted (he built and paid for
this home for her)(and planned to move her away forever)
successful (he left her much money)(to spend in California)
and famous (his name and face were distributed
throughout the middle west on bottles
of his patent medicine)
Doctor Hozier

Just because they said she was stand-offish
(and a bit peculiar)
(and maybe unneighborly)
I was not supposed to hang around her place
as often and as thoroughly as I desired
(Just because they said such intriguing things)
She would motion to me to come set awhile
and (together) we would admire her hollyhocks
and her candytuft, her sweet william,
and her freesias,
and we would talk
and (mostly) she would tell me how bad
kids had come to be
(the current younger generation) (mine)
about how they were being turned out worse
about how they were turning out worse
all the time
and I would nod and speculate (cheerful)
(but not out loud)

Just because she wore an aura utterly unique
and made me feel close to her superiority
and the unmentioned mysteries of her private living
and not necessarily because I could have agreed
with her dismal apprehensive vistas
I felt small-boy secure upon her enclosed porch
and in her fierce shy unneighborhood presence
and opinion did not matter much at all
amid the (taste it!) lovely scent of candytuft
and the thick wicker luxury of her rocking chairs

Just because they whispered of her past
and of her winning of the mysterious (was he
a real MD?) doctor, late, her spouse
because they whispered weird and wonderful whispers
and they conjured up a presence
(far more real)
of an imagined
great evil-doer
it bristled
in my imagination
more than Treasure Island
it was almost as scary as a Fu Manchu
these whispers conjured up (con man!) configurations
and weird unworded etceteras (in my head)
more exciting than anything anyone said
about any other neighbor

Just because she was the first real confidant
I ever had on my own
(even though most of what
I said to her
I only said in my head)
she was the only one I knew who used
so many clean old lace squares and odds and ends
on upholstered and wicker arms of her chairs
tired old turkish and porch rockers alike
and they were held pin neat (with neat pins)
and she, holding court, let me be
all her noblemen
her counts and her knights and her special court jester

LEADER

He is still the leader / in a new situation / it is always so with him /
he eats up old situations / he is obviously the leader / every exciting
gesture / smile / word / every inch / of him / he laughs like concentrated sunshine
breaking the laws of / physics / (as easily as he breaks the laws of men)
it is part of the dramatic event he produces / every moment / which is
himself masked / or (rather) is himself masked / masked

He is a natural leader / the guys look up to him / the young ladies look /
at him / in a more direct / less psychological way / he is handsome gentle soft
strong rugged charming bright and black / his hair is kinky thick / and always
a little dusty / his eyes shine / whether with a clearness / or a glazed
hung-over condition / depending on who is / looking / and in his eyes / it is always
in his eyes / his small boy grown large / his sexual-dishevelled look

His tragedy is a terrible excess of good looks
a poor beaten small uneducated unforceful drunken papa
a strong domineering educated (after she successfully fought / to raise
feed and launch a family) / self-possessed dynamo of a mama / and a secret
real and unexpected inferiority complex / (he hides the enormity of his
shortcomings / to himself / dramatizing himself as cool / dauntless / a giant
of a leader / and he is (a little) insane

His tragedy is that his papa is not so beaten / as he makes him out to be
and his mama is someone altogether different / from the idea / to the simple
facts of her / the mama he mourns / and the mama who bore him / bear no
resemblance / at all

Perhaps it is his tremendous mind capacity / playing tricks / within himself
causing him to dig causes / and people / situations / and challenges
and dangers / to dig the imaginary / alike with the real / perhaps it is the man
who remains the boy / unbearably aware / he is not reaching for / his real potential

Perhaps it is the game / playing chicken / with himself / being a living
brinksman / always on the edge of desperation / feeling with a ghastly horror
in an agonizing invisibility / the sword / poised within short death distance
of his own neck

It is the beautiful boy / looking with disgust / in the mirror of his own
mind / saying: I'll destroy you / little brother / mother / fake / fake / fake
goddamn uncle tom / poor cheap phoney / nigger / *scared* nigger
He drinks like it might result in an unbearable look / into himself
if he lets up / for a moment / too long / which is what has happened
(desperation) / during sentences served / in hospitals / in jails /
and he cannot stand / the sight of / "the leader" / which is what he calls
himself / acid with sadness / poison with loathing

The leader is convincing / knows how to say / exactly / what is most
desired of him / by the lady who is paying / tonight's bar / and then bottle
and (maybe) bed / bill / desired by the group / who hire him / to lead them
desired by the ideology that he digs a little intellectually (only
intellectually) / who he is pleased with / when he knows they are sure / losers
dependably / proven so / losers / so he will never be tested

On some late night occasions / he calls an old / and trusted (though
discarded) friend / and tells her / anonymously / that he has died / and she's
supposed to weep hysterically / saying: how brilliant! / how good! /
how marvelous he was! / and she is supposed to bemoan / such a sad /
such tremendous waste / this shock call in the middle of the night / has worked
several times / until the shock / wears off / for good

Everything works / no matter how ridiculous / unbelievable / everything works
several times / and everything / (eventually) / stops working / in spite of
his small boy bottom / in spite of his innocent / split / (near the zipper)
britches / in spite of his raucous / epidemic laugh / in spite of him
everything stops / because of him / and he is building in / securely /
his own death / insuring the waste / of his own / so superior / resources
just like in a very bad / play / he so loves to dramatize / into bar mirror
which is his greatest / depth / to date.

SO DON'T BLAME ME

My dear darling precious child
I **know**
you are as good
as anyone
So don't blame **me**
if you stay drunk
if you fail to see your true
potentiality
Don't blame your father either
for both he and I
(who raised you)
see in you
all there needs to be
for you to develop into something special
You **are** *bright*
you do not **need** *to drink*
Don't use me as your excuse
I know you do not need to drink
not just because
your mother is a drunk
I **know**
I asked a doctor
Alcoholism is not
hereditary
So **don't** *blame me. . .*

THE BEST TIMES

The best times about being young
were being sick
(or pretending) (a match and
a thermometer)
(a thermometer is not match
to a lit match)
when she sympathized
fluffed pillows
served cambric tea
and chicken broth to me in bed
and read
and read
reading fantasy and verse
and when she read Stevenson
and I became the Kings
and conquered cabbages
and my mind moved through
storybooks
and her love for me
came through
The best times about being young
were being sick
when she was not sick too. . .

IS THERE ACCOUNTABILITY?
I'm told things I can
not forget!

They gave Abbie Hoffman hepatitis in Washington, C.C.
in the filth of a federal jail cell
and they called that justice
just as Adolph Hitler
legally injected
death to anyone
distasteful to
the 1000–year Reich

They gave Abbie Hoffman a distaste for the United States of CIA
Did I say distaste? Or was it a bellyache?
Or was it hepatitis of the spirit?
Was it legal lynch justice?
Was it successful?
Did it work?

NO.

So they brought idealist loving–clown Abbie
Youth volunteer for civil rights
Young seeker–activist for justice
Advocate of love
(Wrong only for right reasons)
They brought Abbie to their stinking justice dozens of times
and he always appeared
seeking the myth of justice in his native land
and they couldn't nail him
in their elaborate
legal coffin

And they tried time after time to get him
and their evil money–energy
their money–power was inexhaustible!
Then the Secret Government
CIA–Mafia–Invisible 40–Super–Powerstructure
who stayed on top of Abbie Hoffman
everywhere all the time
except in bed with Anita
They invented a two–pound
senseless unsale of cocaine
to lie to
to misinform America's generous heart
to confuse this (lesser) cocaine invention
with the hidden government of CIA (and all that!)'s
immeasurable horror of heroin
extra–governmental heroin
ace–in–the–hole–money heroin!
GI coffins–full of heroin
CIA plane–loads of heroin
billions and billions and billions of blood dollars
beyond accountability!!!
Partnership in heroin–slavery with the evil hard–drug Mafia
and murder and torture, blackmail and corruption
everywhere in the service of secret government profiteers!

They framed Abbie in the midst of their soulless heroin flood
They framed Abbie as would-be exploiter by way of an imaginary
two-pound sale to their ever-present all-too-visible presence
They framed Abbie who gave all of his one-book success grubstake
to free on bail one brother thus foiling only one spare-no-expense
frame-up! They tried to rob Abbie of his right to be
and Abbie was forced to skip, to go underground
to give up on democracy and freedom and hopes and belief
and they destroyed (or at least got rid of)
the clown-prince of revolutionary love
(accurately reported in factual, prize-winning NEW YORKER magazine)
So this time the super collusive secret government of CIA (and all
that!) succeeded in getting rid of Abbie
as surely as they shot Wallace out of Nixon's essential presidential
path / They got rid of Abbie whose faults were forgivable
but whose love was not
and we all lost

The destruction of their liar-in-chief, horror-bomber-in-chief Nixon
followed closely by the chief manipulators, was or was not triggered
by their intelligence plant / Is the White House man who was quickly
appointed CAB head in order to cover up commercial airliner
disasters that got rid of living threats (such as bag-woman, Mrs. Hunt)
was he with long electronic ears in the White House the one
supposed to light that tape time-bomb? (Jackal Nixon came within inches
of dictatorship) (String-pullers don't like a puppet to try to
take over!) In any case, nobody could double-cross the secret
government of CIA (and all that!), certainly not their next man
in the White House Offal office, for that used Ford we bought from
the crooked used-car salesman had acted as a chief cover-up architect
in the outrageous Warren Commission / So we cannot find out the
multinationals' role in the secret government, or who engineered
the presidential assassination, or who the murderers were!
We are allowed a let's-pretend a little longer if we are
the easily fooled fools they think we are!

But Abbie Hoffman won't stay dead, and May Brussel and company
won't shut up! Their voices freeze our blood! Their volumes of
files, their thousands of facts, their years of carefully-
researched conspiracy links and acts and the deadly pattern
won't go away! They won't go away. Will we demand answers?
The horrible revelations prove to be right too often!
Abbie is become like a rash in the American heart as the dream
keeps growing into a nightmare that won't let up or stop
and belief in force and violence and people's revolutionary bosses
threatens liberty inside our heads
Does Abbie believe yet in a someday love
perhaps imposed love in an authoritarian future?

Has Abbie lost faith in the triumph of an American dream
that once was ALL loving and libertarian?
Has Abbie lost the possibility of a new human loving
giving life-style!
Abbie is carrying on whatever beliefs may be left for him
in an atmosphere of potential violence
in the American underground
Abbie is still fighting an America manipulated
by a CIA (and all that!) everywhere secretly present
with brain-implant assassin teams out of prison and asylum violence
with mental hospital manufactured zombies
our now-endless Night of the Living Dead!

And Abbie is at our mercy
and WE are at our mercy
for we know we are all under fire now
and the 40-times-Mister-X and Reagan-Rockefeller-Ford and
multinational Gangster-dope-CIA Profiteer protection racketeers
consolidate their gigantic power unloyal to any people
Power against all people except the most powerful!

Is Abbie right?
Are we all dupes and fools and is torture the new wave
and are we buying the phoney freedom proclaimed by
unbridled world-wide Profits Pirates?
And is assassination the American way at home
and in other lands?
Is assassination now our continuing, unbeatable, all-consuming basis?
Is Abbie right?
Or is he and are the full-time researchers of the conspiracy,
May Brussell and the others,
Are they wrong?
Or are we?
all of us who love the gentle way,
all the way wrong?

I have no answer.
Does anyone?
Can we start to stop this totally corrupt corporate state
before it is too late?
Can we register but REFUSE to vote
and then refuse to pay taxes
and refuse to be raped by the evil of money-power-greed?
Can we lovingly, non-violently revolt?
Or must we too shriek one day soon from ITT's expert electro-
genital torture
and from CIA (and all that!) electrode brain-implants
directing murder?

Will we continue to allow them to continue to dispose of
any freedom that may get in their way?
Are we all Teddy Kennedy (rightly) in terror for our lives?
Are we all facing UNBEATABLE billions (or trillions)
of conscienceless power
to shut off our humanity?
Is Teddy Kennedy the living symbol of our death?
Is Abbie's worst fear our living hell?

Who can answer?

Are we hiding?
Is America's heart shut up?
Will truth out?
Can truth out?
Can we set us free?
Is there yet an American myth about the worth of each one?
Or is it merely the enormous hidden evil's cover story?
Does the dream of Walt Whitman and Lao Tze and Jesus and
Tom Paine still live?
Or is there mostly an American filth
determined to out-Hitler the memory of Hitler?

Is the United States of CIA (and all that) to go on pulling
the strings attached to our greatest vulnerabilities?
Are the CIA etc. and the American Money-God
going to get away with dousing the American spirit with
slave-bait both heroin and media mind-management?
Will we let them get away with the destruction of
those ideas of human decency we tried to believe?
Or are we polluted beyond reviving
even before the great oil death kills our oceans
and we slowly suffocate for lack of renewed oxygen from
plant life in the oceans?

Abbie, is yours the only answer?
And you, heart of America, do you care enough now
even though it is almost too late?

I AM ASKING MYSELF.

*I insist the individual is the root of all social life
The individual commands my first respect
unless another be precisely hurt
the one is free to act or not
as she/he sees fit
and this is it
society is you and me
and we are the base of power
not the farthest bottom away
I insist one "single, separate person" contains all
rights, benefits, consideration, and all respect
and any society not so oriented is an enemy of
the people and I insist this libertarianism–anarchism
works because it is so right.*

SUPER BLUE

They sneaked sex back into Connecticut
in large
friendly
free-travelling
balloons
painted dangerous colors
and filled with true
blue
super helium

Sex flowed
over the purple people
high
over the purple people

They sneaked sex back into Connecticut
and Jersey marshes
and far up into Ottawa
without anyone
anywhere
down
knowing what to do
about it

But the people who sampled
the sex that flew
have learned how
to fly
their own!

AFTERTHOUGHT

And what <u>they</u> think
   of what I think of it,
Or what <u>they</u> think
      I think
(if they think I think at all)
Is not going to occupy
   a moment of my thought.

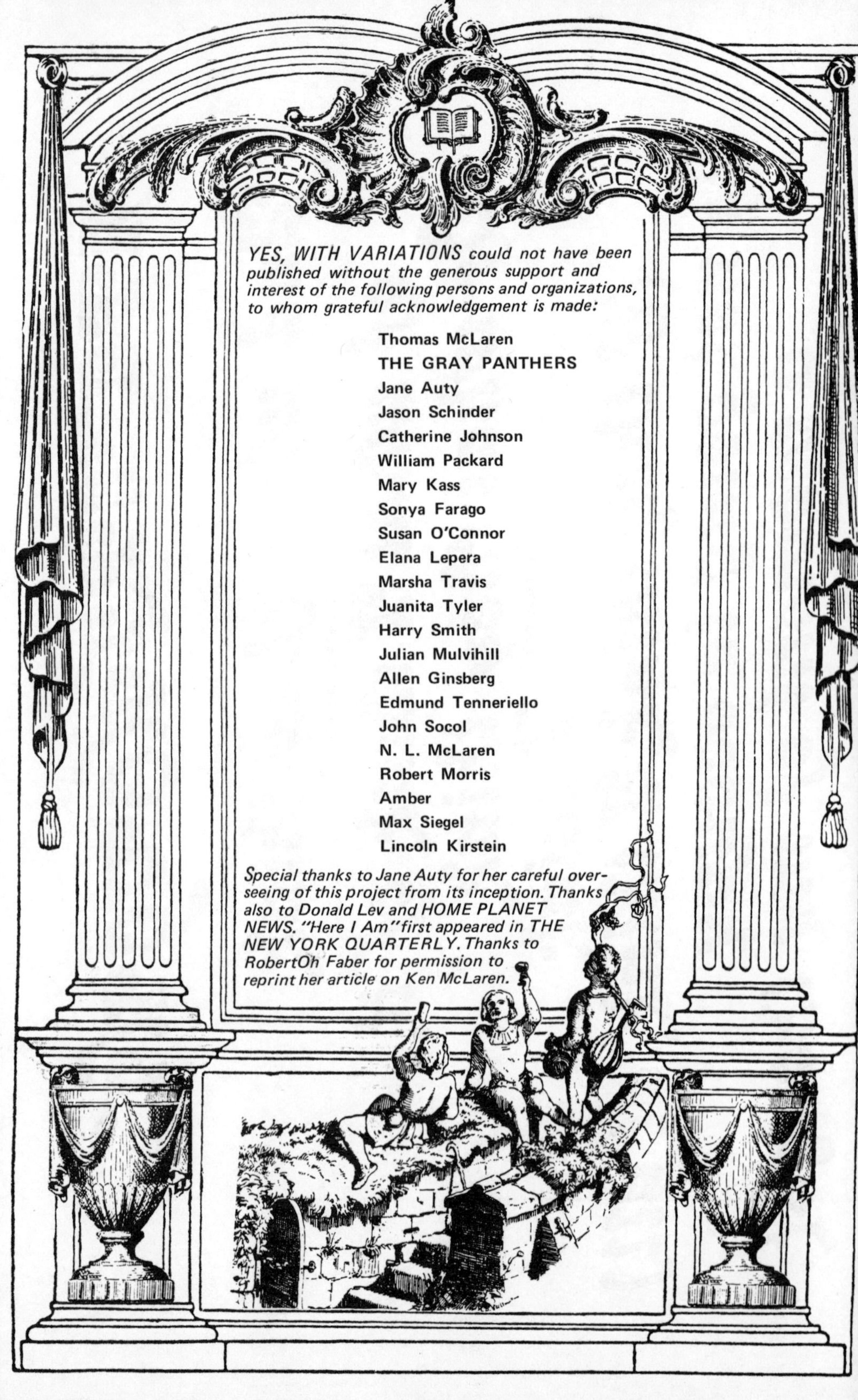

YES, WITH VARIATIONS could not have been published without the generous support and interest of the following persons and organizations, to whom grateful acknowledgement is made:

Thomas McLaren

THE GRAY PANTHERS

Jane Auty

Jason Schinder

Catherine Johnson

William Packard

Mary Kass

Sonya Farago

Susan O'Connor

Elana Lepera

Marsha Travis

Juanita Tyler

Harry Smith

Julian Mulvihill

Allen Ginsberg

Edmund Tenneriello

John Socol

N. L. McLaren

Robert Morris

Amber

Max Siegel

Lincoln Kirstein

Special thanks to Jane Auty for her careful overseeing of this project from its inception. Thanks also to Donald Lev and HOME PLANET NEWS. "Here I Am" first appeared in THE NEW YORK QUARTERLY. Thanks to RobertOh Faber for permission to reprint her article on Ken McLaren.